FROM MY HEART TO YOURS!:
Uplifting Poetry from Betty Lee

Betty Lee Fulop

SUNSET
INSTITUTE PRESS
3710 34th, Lubbock, TX

All scripture is taken from the King James
Version of the Bible.

ISBN 978-0-9846460-9-8

For orders, please send $6.95 plus $2.55
for shipping and handling to:

Poetry From Betty Lee
4064 Sunset Road
Athol, Idaho (ID) 83801-9206

Information on orders of more than one book call
208-699-8738 or e-mail me at:
poetryfrombettylee@yahoo.com

www.bettyleefulop.com

Note to the Reader:

I have shared my poetry with others for over twenty-five years, and many have urged me to get them into print. I am thrilled that the time for that has come. I have, however, seen the need to make changes in a number of the poems.

I cannot claim sole authorship for these writings, because I learned in 1985 that God had given me the wonderful gift for writing poetry. Therefore, I feel these poems are "from" me, not "by" me.

The poems herein were born out of many experiences, such as: when I was in prayer, while "into" the Bible, when I was out for a walk viewing God's glorious nature and talking with him, or when I was depressed. Some were therapy for me as I healed from various types of abuses received over a period of some sixty years.

I pray this book of poetry will honor my Father, the God of heaven, and His Son, Jesus, to whom I have given my life and my allegiance. I also pray your heart will be touched and your life richly blessed, for these poems are truly from my heart—and I send them forth to you on the wings of prayer.

Betty Lee Fulop
January 5, 2012

I

Acknowledgement:

First and foremost, I give praise and thanksgiving to my Father in heaven who gave me the wonderful gift for writing the kind of poetry you see in this book. I am most grateful for the many people who encouraged me over the years to publish these poems, and for those who helped in various ways to improve the writing of them. All have been valuable contributions.

Most of all, I am greatly indebted to those dear souls in Lubbock, Texas, who helped with this book of poetry: Nell Brady, who proofread the manuscript, and Richard Cravy and Virgil Yocham, who prepared the manuscript for printing. Also, I appreciate so much and thank my friend Mollie Ryan of Coeur d'Alene, Idaho and my nephew's wife, Caralee Harkins of Wyoming, Michigan, for the hours spent in finding errors in the two proof copies needed to help make this book as good as it is.

Dedication:

This book of poetry is dedicated to the students at Harding University (HU) in Searcy, Arkansas who are in the Center for Advanced Ministry Training (CAMT) program. It was my pleasure to attend their chapel services during my last year at HU and I came to love them dearly.

Where Jesus Walked

Oh! To think I soon shall walk
in Israel! Yes! There abroad
In that now troubled spot on earth
where once my Savior trod.

Oh! To think that I shall stand
in the Garden of Gethsemane
Where Jesus prayed before He died
on the cross for you and me!

Oh! To think that I shall see,
with joy filling my heart,
The hills, the towns, the very Sea
in which Jesus played a part.

Oh! How I pray that I shall be
intrigued by things that matter,
As I walk the roads that Jesus walked
with His friends midst talk and chatter.

And when these days of travel are o'er
and life is busier than ever,
Dear Jesus, continue to walk with me
each day in every endeavor.
Miss Betty

*(Written October 18, 2011 for the CAMT students
who will visit Israel in 2012 for the first time.)*

IV

CONTENTS

VIII

<u>Introduction</u>

I Am a Poet

I am a poet
And I know it
Little else I want to be;
Words that rhyme
Rhythm, time,
Wondrous things they do for me!

~~~~~~~~~~

Let me introduce myself—
My name is Betty Lee;
I like to do a lot of things,
But most of all write poetry.

It's a Poet's
Life

I daily live and daily breathe
in meter and in rhyme;
I think of putting all my thoughts
in poem form—all
the time!

I thank my friends and family
for putting up with me,
For when they visit they must hear
my latest poetry.

1

Life Without A Poem?

Life—without some poetry?
Dear friend, don't wish that life for me.
I need a little jingle, rhyme,
To make me smile from time to time;
A jolly song with flair and art;
Encouraging words to lift my heart;
A poem to comfort and to bless;
A poem to help in times of stress;
A poem of thought to make me think;
A psalm of praise that's like a drink;
Some pointed verse to make me weep;
Some solemn words that go down deep
Into the very depth of soul
To help me reach a higher goal.

Oh yes, that is the life for me:
Rich blessings from good poetry.

Relationships

They are everywhere, on every hand,
Wherever you turn throughout the land!
And they were here when I came to earth;
Now, as I grew *they* grew, giving "birth"—
Becoming more, until you see,
They've overwhelmed and engulfed
poor me.

Creative

Works of God

Thou art worthy, O Lord,
to receive glory and honour and
power: for thou hast created
all things, and for thy pleasure
they are and were created.

Revelation 4:11

Come, Laugh and Love With Me

Come, laugh with me of funny things,
of silly things, and be
Not always weighed or loaded down
with worried thoughts. You see,
A hearty laugh or belly laugh
will do you good! For God *did* say
That laughing is good medicine,
so come and laugh away!

Come, love with me the things God made,
the blue, the lovely green,
And all the creatures and the good
He sandwiched in between.
Come, see the birds, the animals,
the smiles of children dear,
And love each thing our Maker made,
and really live while here.

Come, laugh and love and taste of life
and seek the better way;
Did not our Maker make you fine?
Does He not keep each day?
Did He not set within the heart
a need to laugh and love?
Then come, and laugh and love with me
to please our God above!

My View of God's Animals

God made some funny animals
So we could laugh and smile, I know;
He made some strong and husky ones,
And some that flutter, crawl, and glow.

God made the elk and graceful deer,
The many creatures of the sea;
He made the big cats and the bears,
And soft and cuddly ones for me.

God made some animals to be
Used on the farm; and then to fly
And sing, God made those lovely birds
That transforms both the earth and sky.

Creatures of the Sea

Ugly or most beautiful,
gigantic or quite small;
Wonderfully made are they
with arms or none at all;
Praise the mighty God of heaven
who made for you and me
Amazing and magnificent
creatures of the sea.

God's Creation

God made the lovely animals,
the birds and butterflies,
With hair or feathers, wings (or not),
with ears and teeth and eyes,
And humps and bumps and funny legs,
and faces—some so queer;
Yet don't you think each animal
is awesome, great, or dear?
God made each one uniquely and,
for each one now we say,
"Oh, Thank you God, for animals;
we praise Your work today."

The Little
Gifts

The birth of a flow'r from the tiniest seed,
The power of healing from herb and its seed;
The beauty we oft see on bright colored wing,
The peace of the ev'ning when small crickets sing,
The sun shining down on a blue-jeweled lake,
The great way we feel when from sleep we awake;
The smiles and the laughter of little children,
Embraces so warm from both friends and
close kin—

The list of these gifts from the Father to me
Is endless and wondrous, and surprisingly free.

Snow Upon the Pine

A sunset is quite beautiful
and mountain lakes the same;
And animals and plants and birds,
God's creatures wild and tame.

(Also the new and great ideas
upon man's mortal mind),
But nothing is as pretty
As fresh snow upon the pine.

The Awesome Sight

I looked about and saw a tree
of great and massive size,
Whose beauty took my breath away
and brought tears to my eyes.
A saw there in its trunk and leaves
the Maker's Sovereign hand,
And thanked him for such beauty that
He'd spread through out the land.
I cared not that another saw
The tears stream down my face,
I only marveled at the pow'r
of God in that tree's grace.

The First Six Days

In the beginning was nothing.
Nothing at all!
'Til God in His power created
the earth like a ball.

I

The earth had no form, and the darkness
was spread o'er the deep;
Then God's Spirit moved o'er the waters,
and God rose to speak,
"LET THERE BE LIGHT!" and the darkness
was scattered away,
For light was poured out o'er the world
to make the first day.

II

A firmament God made the next day,
to simply divide
The waters above from the waters below,
then God cried,
"LET THE WATERS BE GATHERED TOGETHER,
AND DRY LAND APPEAR!"
So the waters that flowed under heaven,
out over the sphere
Were gathered together in one place,
and God called them Seas;

9

III

Then dry land appeared on that third day,
but there were no trees—
Only mountains and valleys and seashores
with wide empty plains;
So God wisely brought forth good grasses
And wonderful grains,
And beautiful flowers and fruit trees,
and herbs yielding seed,
And planted each lovely creation,
where there was a need.

IV

"NOW, LET THERE BE LIGHTS IN
THE HEAVENS!"
Our God then cried out;
So huge, heavenly bodies, abundant,
well-fixed and quite stout
Were set in position, with great lights,
the moon and the sun,
To rule and divide light from darkness;
then day four was done.

V

Then out o'er the waters God called out
for creatures to be
Brought forth in mighty abundance
to fill up the sea.
That fifth day he made lovely winged fowl
of beautiful hue

To nest in the trees, rocks, and meadows—
and soar in "the blue."

VI

Then—glory and power resplendent were in
great display
When God made the great and small creatures
That glorious sixth day.
Amazing and wonderful creatures
our God did create,
Crowning His labor—so perfect—
with man and his mate!

God blessed man and said, "Oh, be fruitful;
replenish the earth,
Subdue it and have the dominion
o'er all that gives birth!"
And God saw each day His creation,
and proudly He stood
Looking down with great joy and much pleasure,
And cried out, "IT'S GOOD!"

Look Again

When you look at God's creation
What do you see?
Forest? Field?
Mountain?
Sky, land, and sea?

11

Do you see animals?
Birds? Insects?
Marine life *and* people?

Look again.
Do you see the intricate patterns
The minute designs
The varied shapes
The many and beautiful hues
The moves and personalities?

Look again.
Do you see the power
The awesomeness of the creator
In the majesty of a tree
The strength of a horse
The beauty of a flower
The depth of the ocean?

Do you see His loving kindness
In the sparkling, cool waters
In the warmth of the sun
The healing of a wound?

Do you see His humor
    in the funny looking creatures?
His tenderness in the smile of a baby?
His longsuffering with man's indecision
    and wavering faith!?

Look yet again.
See a glorious and holy,
yet merciful God
Who made man in His image,
Who had a plan—
And *still* has a plan *and* a purpose
For each created individual
With rewarding consequences,
If only we, through faith,
Choose to look and see again.

God Made Them for a Reason

Now bugs abound in earth and ground
(We all take this for granted)
Yet oft we say, what good are they?
They gobble things I've planted!

Though worms and bugs don't need our hugs
They need respect and direction
For some good use and not abuse
In every corner and section.

Our God above in knowing love
Put bugs here for a reason,
So let's employ those bugs with joy
In every time and season.

Idaho, The Beautiful

Oh Idaho, the beautiful,
　　Oh land of endless dream;
The beauty of your varied lands
　　Give many an eye a gleam.
Oh state of gems, of forests, lakes,
　　of rivers blue and green;
Of rugged mountains, rolling hills,
　　You're the prettiest I have seen.

A playground for the sportsman,
　　The hunter's paradise;
The nature lover's classroom,
　　Delight for tourists' eyes.
No matter when or how or where
　　I travel through your state,
A smile comes quite naturally—
　　Because I think you're great!

Flowers

Beauty on bushes up high or down low,
Sweet smelling fragrance wherever I go;
　　What comfort and healing
　　for sorrow and pain
Comes through their great beauty,
　　again and again.

The Mighty

God Above

God is greatly to be feared in
the assembly of the saints, and to
be had in reverence of all them
that are about him.

Psalm 89:7

The God Who Lives Above

Now some folks think Almighty God
hears not our ev'ry plea,
That "He's too busy with the world
for little folk like me."
But God, who lives in heav'n above,
though GREAT, oft bends quite low
To handle simple, little things;
He's helped me thus, I know.

In little things as well as big
I've seen His pow'rful hand,
And trusted Him through many years,
So now for Him I'll stand.
I know this God is there for me
whene'er I need His care,
He's there for ev'ry little thing,
each hour and everywhere.

And so I give my all to Him,
this God who lives above;
For he's a God of grace and hope,
a God of truth and love.
He waits to hear me pray and ask
for help in time of need,
Then gladly bends with mercy great
to satisfy and lead.

What it Takes

It takes *time* to get a relationship going,
Good *communication* to keep it flowing,
Honesty and *love* to keep it glowing;
And with God it takes a lot of *knowing*!

Today I Saw God

Today I saw God in the form of a flower,
In the shape of a leaf, some fruit in a bower;
Today I heard God, but I also could see
Him laugh (through a child),
then He smiled at me.

Today I felt God, and I knew He was real
For I learned of His power and His love I
could feel;
Today I have sensed that my Jesus was near
For a servant of His had in love
brought me cheer.

Today I saw God in the kindness of one
Who met a great need, thus God's service was
done;
So there is no doubt that this God really lives,
And through Christ and His Spirit
He loves and He gives.

He is There
for Me

God the greatest Monarch,
To whom I bow my knee,
Lord of heaven and Lord of earth,
Yet He is there for me!

Ruler of the heaven's
Is His Majesty,
Yet He, my Heavenly Father,
Loves being there for me!

Mightier than the ocean,
Mightier than the sea
Is God, my God in heaven;
What joy! He's there for me!

Lover of my heart and soul,
Is Christ who made me free,
And like my Heavenly Father
He's always there for me!

A Great
Need

The need to obey what the scriptures say
must ever be emphasized;
For the word of the Lord is to be adored
and never minimized.

The Book of
Promises

There's a book of holy promises
for those who live on earth;
A book for both the sinner
and the saint of greatest worth.

It tells us of an action
that will wash our sins away;
It tells us of a power
that is ours to claim each day.

It states that we can please the One
who loves us with great love;
It gives us full assurance
from the Father's throne above.

It comforts us in sorrow great,
it strengthens us in pain;
It gives a hope that brings a song,
a wondrous, sweet refrain.

This book is called the Bible
and its promises are rife;
Its words are from the God above
who gives eternal life.

He spoke to holy men of God
Through His glorious Holy Spirit,
Who gave to man God's promises
of grace and love and merit.

Praise God this book of promises
was given you and me;
Praise God He gave this book to us
so we could faithful be.

God Changes Not

God changes not;
I must each day.
He need not change;
I must always.
God stays the same both day and night,
Full of mercy, love and might.

His heart for man's
redemption yearns;
From faithfulness
He never turns.
He'll help us with our ev'ry need,
Whene'er before His throne we plead.
Praise God He changes not, but I?
I must change and for it cry.

21

The Tower Strong

God's glorious Name is a holy tower,
A safe abode, a grace-filled bower;
It's a place where strivings all will cease,
For there abides God's lasting peace.

God's holy Name has might and power
And stands above ev'ry other tower;
It stands above all wrong and right
To strengthen Christians day and night.

Dear God

How I love all Your
marvelous workings
Your wonders
Your righteous ways
and Your glorious truth.

How I enjoy the way
You bring surprises
knowledge
comfort
joy
pleasure
and enlightenment
to the longing soul.

Every minute of every day
I appreciate and need
Your love
peace
mercy
grace
strength and power.

Through Your wonders
of love and power
that work in, through
and around me
You lift me up
build me up
hold me close
teach me
guide me
assure me of Your love
and bring me to my knees.

From the depth
of my heart
and soul
I thank You.
You are Divine Love
and I praise
Your holy Name
For who You are
And what You do.

O God

If You should mark iniquities
and give us all our due,
No one could stand before You, Lord,
or find salvation true;
For all have sinned and all fall short
of Your glory and Your grace;
And if Jesus lives not in our hearts
we'll never see Your face.

Thank You Father God

I know not what today will bring,
I only know that I should sing
And praise You for my life; so now
Before Your throne I humbly bow
And give You glory for the way
You've been with me from day to day.

God's Gift of Love

God had a wondrous gift for man,
but waited many years
To give this gift, while man lived on
in hope and sometimes tears.
Then when the time was right and good,
God sent His only Son

To fight the greatest fight of all—
with Satan—and He WON!
So now we, too, can win the fight
o'er Satan, self, and sin,
If we let Jesus be our guide
and His Spirit reign within.

I Wonder

I wonder if God,
over 2,000 years ago
felt inner excitement
when it was time for Jesus
to come to earth.

He had planned it,
prepared the world for it,
longed for it to happen.
Now it was time.

What joy!
What love went into
this wonderful gift
He gave the world.

Jesus, born under the law,
born of a woman,
the only begotten Son of God,
Savior of sinful man.

Heavenly Help

My Heavenly Father
    As any Father should do
        Very tenderly
           Lovingly
              Gradually
                 Purposely
Guides me on and through
    The problems of life.

Slowly, with the Spirit's help
    I'm growing in grace and knowledge
        Fighting
           Losing
              Winning
                Walking
And sometimes running—the race
    Set before me.

Looking unto Jesus
    The Author and Finisher of our faith
        Believing
           Trusting
              Praying
                Serving
No longer a wayward, hopeless waif
    But headed for home.

Jesus,

God's Son and

our Savior

For God sent not his Son into

the world to condemn the world;

but that the world through

him might be saved.

John 3:17

God's Miracle of Love

He came.
God's miracle came
from heaven above;
Born of woman,
wrapped in a blanket of love.

He lived.
An example of love
and right was He;
Against all sin He fought,
our Lord to be.

He died.
He offered himself
as sacrifice;
As payment for our sins
He was the price.

He arose!
And ascending to God's
holy throne above
He became King Jesus,
God's miracle of love.

J - E - S - U - S

J ust a Jew to many, but

E verything to me;

S acrifice so excellent,

U ltimate authority.

S avior to believers,
   making many free.

Power in Jesus' Name

I know there's power in Jesus' name,
The scriptures tell me so;
I know He heals and keeps and saves,
Yes, this I truly know.

There's power when we say 'thank you'
And praise and magnify
His name above all other names,
This One who lives on high.

There's power when we speak His name,
When Satan tempts us sore;
Yes, power when we ask His help
To love Him more and more.

Why Jesus Came

He came to be the TRUTH, the WAY,
To be the needed LIGHT;
He came to be our CAPTAIN true,
To help us in the fight.

He came to vanquish Satan's hold,
To get the upper hand;
He came to tell each burdened soul
There is a better land.

He came to be our RIGHTEOUSNESS,
To rid each heart of sin;
He came, the best EXAMPLE yet
Of how to live and win!

He came to be our great HIGH PRIEST,
To help us when we pray;
He came the holy BREAD of God,
Sustaining us each day.

He came THE RESURRECTION—yes!
Thank God we now can be
Hopeful while in Christ we live,
headed for eternity.

Shout It!

Shout it from the mountain top,
Shout it from the plain;
God's Son came down from heaven
to earth
Then went to heaven again.

He went to heaven to be our King
Our Lord, our Advocate;
He sits to rule the hearts of those
Who enter Kingdom's Gate.

Now all who live in Christ, rejoice!
God's Son in heaven lives!
And in each heart is spread God's love
By the Spirit that He gives.

So shout it from the mountain top,
And shout it from the plain,
God lives and loves in those who give
Themselves to Him again, again.

Listen Please

I want to sing, I want to shout,
"This life's not all there is.
There's more, there's more,
the soul dies not,
Beyond the grave it lives!"

His Love Does
it All

The love Christ has for me
(not my love for Him)
draws
compels
and moves me
to tears, action and
thanksgiving.

The love Christ has for me
(not my love for Him)
saves
strengthens
and constrains me
to remain close to Him
in faithfulness.

The love "Christ has for me
(not my love for Him)
fills
fulfills
and persuades me
to share His love and
to magnify His name.

Jesus, the Shepherd, We the Sheep

In the morning of our Christian lives
He leads us out to feed
Upon the green grass of His word,
and oh, so gently leads
Us into places and in ways
that satisfy our needs,
So we can live our lives for Him
in truth and word and deed.

At noontime when the day is bright
He brings us to the stream,
Where we can drink the waters of
His living word supreme.
And oh, we think it is His best,
but no, in God's great scheme
He's furnished endless blessings rich
for those Christ did redeem.

Then comes the time when we no more
have thoughts to bulk or stray;
Each time He calls we come to Him,
there is no long delay.
We follow as He guides us
and we long to see the day
When we go home to be with Him,
and there forever stay.

But while we're here we live each day
as if it were our last,
and look into the future, thus
forgetting all the past.
We know the joy unspeakable,
the peace of God so vast;
We are so ever grateful for
His love so strong and fast.

Oh, yes! We are so much like sheep!
He is our Shepherd dear;
He loves and knows us each by name,
and wants to keep us near.
He longs to fill our every need
if we will stop and hear
His voice above the other sheep
and never from Him veer.

Jesus, My King

Yes, I am His and He is mine
(Our relationship is quite sublime),
Therefore my heart can truly sing
For Jesus, my Lord, is also my KING.

Just think, I now am royalty!
What better thing could ever be?
But, if *you* are His and thus made "new",
Then He's *your* King; you're royalty, too!

35

And Jesus Is
His Name

Ignorance.
Violence.
Greed.
All these brought darkness and shame;
Then God sent His ray of sunshine,
And JESUS is His name.
Light.
Love.
Righteousness.
This is our Lord, this His **claim;**
He destroyed the powers of darkness,
And JESUS is His name.

At the Foot of
the Cross

At the foot of the cross I see Jesus,
The One who cared much for my soul;
And I stand there with fear
and with trembling
As I look out o'er Calvary's knoll.

Oh! how dearly He paid,
Oh! how much He did bear,
As He hung on the cross,
As He died for me there.

At the foot of the cross I take Jesus
And put Him, in baptism on,
Then rise up to live a grand, new life,
For in Jesus my past sins are gone.

I'm His bond-servant now
And I'll walk in His way,
For I've firmly resolved
By His dear side to stay.

At the foot of the cross I take courage
To surrender my will to my Lord,
For God's mighty power and purpose
Are present, through His Spirit and word.

I praise God for His love!
I'm so thankful to know
That in Jesus I'm safe,
And with me He will go.

Lessons

Great lessons live along the way
Where'er we travel day by day;
We learn the best, I think, from those
Which hit us in the face or nose
Then bid the learning come to rest
Within our hearts, a welcome guest.

Once

The Son of God came once to die,
once to give His life;
Once for sin an offering
to end all shame and strife.

He came to live, He came to die,
obedient was He;
He came to do the Father's will,
our sacrifice to be.

Now interceding daily for
the saved in ev'ry land
Our great High Priest, the King of kings
sits now at God's right hand.

There'll be no other sacrifice,
no other one to die,
No other one to show us how
to live for God on high.

Jesus Loves Them Still

The apple of my Master's eye
are children, young and old;
In mind and body, whole or not,
in spirit warm or cold.

He loves even those who love him not.
He loves, and always will,
For he is God and God is love; yes,
Jesus loves them still.

But what of we who claim to love
the Master, Lord of all,
Yet impart not a love for them,
the children big and small?
When we like Jesus seek to be,
with goals and heart made new,
Then we with holy love aflame
will love the children, too.

A Note From the Lord

It was short.
"My life for yours," it said.
"I gave my flesh, my life,
My all, for you!

"I am the Living Bread;
Take me,
Eat me,
Devour me,
Cherish me
And let me sustain you,
For I am all you need."

As Jesus Lived

Oh, to live as Jesus lived!
Yes, unselfish to the extreme,
Loving others more than self;
This is my want, my dream.

Oh, to talk as Jesus talked!
So gentle, meeting needs,
Telling of God's wondrous love,
Sowing gospel seeds.

Oh, to walk as Jesus walked!
All suffrings gladly bear,
Saying to temptations, "No!"
This is my plea, my prayer.

Oh, to die as Jesus died!
Life's mission, done, complete;
Leaving naught but love behind
When I my Savior meet.

My Journey

of Faith

O LORD, thou hast searched
me, and known me. Thou knowest
my downsitting and mine uprising, thou
understandest my thought afar off.

Psalm 139:1, 2

The Answered
Prayer

The child came, so tired and weak,
"Dear Father, please, mercy I seek.

"This day I've tried so hard to please,
But I have failed…." And on his knees
The child fell. The tears came fast.
The night drew on. The hours passed.

The morning rays of light so fair
Shone down upon the child in prayer,
"Help me to be so strong this day
That I will not t'ward evil stray."

But ev'ning came, and darkness found
The child again, with choking sound,
"I've tried so hard. I'll try some more.
Just give me time, this I implore."

So time was given, and grace was, too.
The child learned, the child grew
In faith, in strength, in grace, in love;
His prayer was answered from above.

Broken

My life was a mess, and I knew it!
I wondered, and often asked, "Why?"
I pleaded, "How long, O my Savior?"
I feared to live on—or to die!

My body was weary with groaning;
My mind, full of woe, was in pain;
I sorrowed and grieved and wept buckets
Of tears, on my bed again, again.

"I'm weak," I cried. "Jesus have mercy!
Please help!" And I fell to the ground;
Broken at last, there repenting;
Broken! with great sobbing sound.

No more do the tears come in buckets;
No more is my life full of woes;
My heart, broken oft, now has mended
And with Jesus' great love overflows.

Slip of the Tongue

I know how very damaging
Vain, thoughtless words can be;
For words slipped far too often
From my fast tongue carelessly.

Touch Me!

Touch me and heal me, O Savior Divine,
Take out the dross from this poor heart of mine.
Take from my heart unbelief; faith increase,
And grant me Thy patience, Thy love, grace
and peace.

Take from my heart all the longing to live
For self and for pleasure, and teach me to give;
I need more devotion, dear Savior—to You!
Please help me each day this desire to renew.

Praise to My Father

O Holy Father, how I praise Thee
For loving me just as I am!
And thank you, too, for cleansing me,
Redeeming by the blood of the Lamb.

O Dearest Father, how I thank Thee
For grace and mercy's ceaseless flow;
For drawing me to Jesus, my Savior,
So I in Him can live and grow.

O Mighty Father, I adore Thee.
Now living free, with Thy Spirit within,
Teach me, lead me, and strengthen greatly
So I'll have vict'ry over sin.

I Know the Victor's Song

Yes! I know what anger is.
> That raging fire from deep within
> That causes many a soul to sin,
> Regretting words and careless ways,
> Then hating self for days and days.

Yes, I know what anger is.

Yes! I know what fear is.
> That crippling force of strong emotion
> Like crashing waves of some deep
> ocean,
> Pounding, lashing o'er my soul
> While life drifts by without a goal.

Yes, I know what fear is.

Yes! I know what guilt is.
> That burdensome, obnoxious foe,
> Producer of the greatest woe,
> Keeping me from wondrous peace
> Because my sin it won't release.

Yes, I know what guilt is.

And yes! Praise God,
I know the victor's song,
> "Set free, set free
> from sin's great power

That kept me chained
each day, each hour;
There, holding me
for many years
Entrenched in anger,
guilt, and fears."

But now I'm free! Thank God I'm free!
Thank you, dear Lord, for saving me.
Praise God! Praise God! I now can say,
"I know the victor's song."

It Paid to Trust in Thee

I waited for the morning, Lord,
As one does needed rain;
For from the depths I cried to Thee
Again, again, again.

My hope was ever present, Lord,
That You would hear my prayer;
I voiced my supplications, for
I needed love and care.

I waited for thy blessings, Lord,
And sure enough they came;
I knew it paid to trust in Thee;
To call upon Thy name.

Don't Give Up on Me

It takes some time, I know, to change,
To give up self, to rearrange
Priorities, to search each thought,
to weigh each motive, as one ought;

And often years and years go by
while brethren shake their heads and sigh.

So don't give up on me, I say,
forgetting for my soul to pray;
For worthwhile changes do come slow,
and I in time *will* change and grow.

If You're Like Me

If you're like me you'll have great dreams,
all for the coming year,
And in your heart—excitement—and
a little bit of fear.
For life is so uncertain and,
you wonder if you'll see
Your dreams take shape and then someday
become reality.

If you're like me those dreams will be
quite bright and great in size,
But you will keep them just the same,
with wonderment and sighs.
For everyone who dreams a lot
will suffer from the pain
Of aching heart because they long
some great thing to attain.

If you're like me I know you'll smile
when thoughts—ideas—come,
And right away I know you'll want
to get to work on some;
Then through your dreams you'll
walk and search
to find a dream or two
That you can take and work to shape
into a goal for you.

If you're like me you'll want to know
where you will fit the best
In God's great plan and ask His help
to give each dream the "test"!
For if it does not then honor Him
and glorify His name,
He'll help you change each yearning dream
so there will be no shame.

Now I Understand

I

I dreamed of having finer things,
Of traveling far and wide;
I thought I'd like a cottage house
With a lakeshore by its side.
I wanted flow'rs and pretty trees
Of every hue and kind,
To put a touch of loveliness
On what I would call mine.

I thought of what I'd do and be
And where I'd go some day;
But only fleeting thoughts had I
Of Jesus and His way.

II

My troubles were of ev'ry kind,
I often asked Him, "Why?"
"What good are all these trials, Lord?"
I'd fight and plead and cry.
For forty years I 'muddled through'
And prayed; life was so dim;
So heavy was my burdened soul,
Yet still I trusted Him.

My dreams by then were growing dim,
No more did I caress

The pleasures of this life, and things;
I thought of self much less.

III

It seems the Lord had better plans
For such a one as I;
He gave me all I needed and
He heard my every cry.
Down through the years he counseled me,
He helped me through my pain.
Now I can comfort other folks,
Oh, Lord, it is so plain!

I understand, oh, praise His name!
Thy goodness, Lord, to me
Was being there, guiding me through;
Thy purpose now I see.

Alone With God

No greater joy I have than this:
Alone with God,
To sense His kiss
Of ardent love upon my brow,
To feel His presence as I vow
To love and honor and obey
His word of truth
From day to day.

On my Knees

At the start of each new day
I'll come to You, O Lord, and pray;
I'll bow before You on my knees.
And seek You Father God to please.

And when the day comes to an end
I'll pray again, my knees I'll bend,
And thank You for Your love and care
That brought me back to You in prayer.

My Heart Will Faithful Be

O God, You know the pain I bear
the unpretentious tear;
You know the intents of my heart
the faith I have, the fear!

Give me the strength to bear the pain,
the faith to beat the fear;
Please keep my heart to love Your word
and hold my Jesus near.

I ask for healing and for truth;
Please Jesus, be with me;
But should You give or should you take
my heart will faithful be.

This World is Not My Home

I'll gladly welcome work and play
That keeps me in the righteous way,
I'll take what comes from God's good hand
And hope above the crowd to stand.

I'll humble self to wait, be still,
To let God bring about His will;
I'll deny self, endure a loss,
And follow Jesus with my cross.

All this because—BECAUSE—you see,
This world is not the home for me.

My home is with my Lord on high,
Where I will go whene'er I die;
This world is just a dwelling place
Where faith is tested by His grace.

My needs will be supplied until
My mission's done and I fulfill
What Jesus has for me to do.
(Just such a mission you have, too!)

All this because—BECAUSE—you see
This world is not the home for me.

Promises

I'm always making promises!
I should by now be smart;
I need to keep my big mouth shut,
Some thoughts within my heart.

But, words slip through unsealed lips!
I need the Spirit's power
To help me put control upon
My tongue and lips this hour.

But, ugly, untrue words seep out!
There is a leak somewhere
And I am forced to call on God
Who makes the best repair.

I know in time I'll hold my tongue,
And this for Jesus' sake;
I'll utter loyal, sincere words
And keep the promises I make.

Change of Plans

God's changed my well-laid plans *again*!
But then I *gave* to Him full reign
Over my life! So now let's see—
Perhaps, perhaps He'll adopt 'Plan B'!

Three Things
I Ask

Dear Jesus, Lord, I have not two
But three small things to ask of you;
I have a blabbering mouth and so
Please do say "yes" and not say "no"
When for a counselor's mouth and ear
I ask; I need to listen, hear.

The matter of the mind is next!
Make mine like Yours so You're
not vexed,
Help me accept the Father's will
And not complain or resent ill;
Then for those trials be prepared
So from correction I'll be spared.

Now last of all, I'd like to see
Two willing hands attached to me;
Yes, willing hands to serve each day,
To shower love in some small way
Upon someone who needs to know
You care for them and love them so.

And let the glory all be Thine,
Who dwells within this heart of mine.

God Works in

His Own

O God, I love Your family,
The ones redeemed by love;
Redeemed by Jesus' precious blood,
Forgiv'n from heaven above.

I know You're working
in their hearts
As each will let You do;
Working out the stubbornness,
Pride and rebellion, too.

I know You're working in Your love,
Your mercy and Your grace;
I know You're working in
their heart,
I can see it on their face!

My Prayer

For ev'ry trial, pain and tear,
As well as blessings of the year,
For home and friends, for food and fun,
And all the things that I have done,
For safety in my travels, too,
For faith and strength the whole year through,
I THANK YOU LORD.

Special for

Christians

But ye are a chosen
generation, a royal priesthood,
an holy nation, a peculiar people...
called out of darkness into
his marvelous light.

I Peter 2:9

Opportunity

Windows are for looking out,
the world to see, to view;
Doors are quite another thing—
they're made for walking through.

If windows you have plenty of,
but doors are very few,
They may be hindering a work
our Lord has just for you.

Let others sit and dream away
through windows big and clear;
Let us seek doors to serve our God
with love and godly fear.

The Key

If you walk and talk with God
in the morning,
Light and bright your mind will grow;
Like smiles on happy children's faces,
Your face may show a distinct glow.

Take twenty minutes with God
in the morning,
Walk and talk and you will see
Your thoughts will clear up very quickly,
For walking and talking is the key.

A Harsh Truth

Love for the world will tarnish the soul,
Steal from the heart every worthwhile goal;
It will take from the mind both peace and joy,
Then give what remains into Satan's employ.

Little Things

'Tis the little things in life that give
that little extra touch
Which brings forth joy and gladness that
we all could use so much.

'Tis the little hug that shows our heart,
that says we really care;
And to make our life worth living,
'tis the little things we share.

'Tis the little gifts that 'spark' the eyes;
and 'tis the humble heart
That kindles motives to be good,
which give us 'push' and 'start.'

'Tis the little need that cries out from
desires deep within,
Which give rise to those little prayers
that keep us from great sin.
'Tis the little deeds we Christian's do

in Jesus' precious name
That brings those extra blessings and
which gives our Jesus fame.

'Tis the little things in life, I know,
that makes each day so grand,
So let us do those little things
and for God's goodness stand.

God Really Cares

When faith loses sight of the
goals ahead
And you know only pain in this
life instead;
When hope vanishes and the
purse is lean
And the joys of this life are
rarely seen,
When trials are sore and the
days seem long
And you know you are weak, when you
should be strong,
Then seek God in His word, you will
find Him there,
For he loves you, My Friend, and He
really does care.

Faith and Fear

Faith and fear can't walk together,
Faith and fear must walk apart;
Faith and fear are much too large
To both at once be in your heart.

But faith is stronger, oh, much stronger
Than fear will ever, ever be:
So put into your heart's vast chambers
God's holy word so fear will flee.

The Bible

Words of light! Oh how I need them;
reaching to the darkened part
Of soul and spirit; but they cut me
like a sword within the heart.

Words of strength! Oh how I want them
when in trials tempted sore;
And how I praise God for their power
as I read to gather more.

Words of grace! Oh what a blessing,
giving hope and mercy great;
Enter now and stay nearby me,
help me on my God to wait.

Words of wisdom! What a treasure,
blessing life from day to day;
Come and waken strong desires,
help me walk the 'Jesus way'.

Dear troubled soul, if you are longing,
for God's power and His grace,
Read, my friend, the Holy Bible;
hear its message, seek God's face.

Stretch

Stretch your soul in daily prayers,
in the reading of God's word;
Stretch your ears to hear the things
that really should be heard.
Stretch your eyes to see the needs
of husband, children, wife,
And of all whom God has given you
to bless your earthly life.

The Love of God

Bask in it.
Warm yourself with it.
Let it grow in you until
It oozes out of you and makes
Beautiful
Everything it touches.

Look Up, Let Go

If peace and joy are strangers,
    and you in spirit are low,
Try looking up to Jesus
    and of yourself let go.

Try seeking godly pleasures
    in tune with Jesus' way;
Try letting go of temporal things,
    that please your house of clay.

Try thanking Him for every pain,
    each heartache and each tear;
Try letting go of failure,
    your worry, and your fear.

Try giving him your disbelief,
    your anger, and your doubt,
Try letting go to see if He
    will turn your life about.

The world is full of faithful souls
    who will to you confess
That Jesus loves and Jesus cares
    and He your faith will bless.

The Proper Time

There's a proper time to meditate,
a proper time to pray;
A time to get responsible,
a proper time to play.
There's a proper time to sit and dream,
a proper time to plan;
A time to take some action and
to do the things you can.

There's a proper time to mourn and weep,
a proper time to sing,
To lift up voice with lilting song,
a joy to others bring.
There's a proper time to think on life,
to re-examine ways,
To strive to keep a balance in
your moments and your days.

There's a time to let go of your fear,
a time to be most glad,
A time to laugh and enjoy life,
to honor Mom and Dad;
There's a time to obey Christ, the King,
the Lord of lords, then give
Your heart and soul to Him, because
He can help you better *live!*

A Matter of Prayer

When trials come and put down roots
and take away your song
So you feel weak in heart and soul
and every things goes wrong;
Remember Jesus loves you and
would daily that you share
Your pain with Him; He'll *listen!*
Just make it a matter of prayer.

When someone slips into a sin
that gives to them and you
A sadness that brings heaviness,
here's what you need to do:
Without a hesitation,
make it a matter of prayer
Give Jesus ev'ry burden and
be sure to leave it there!

When some dear soul reveals to you,
in tones of great disgust,
Another person's sinful side,
with neither love nor trust;
Just say to them in kindness
and a love that shows you care,
"I really think that I should make
this 'sin' a matter of prayer."

When unbelief in someone dear
brings heartache and a tear,
And you have tried to teach them,
yet our God they will not fear;
Please note that God is merciful,
His powerful word can wear
Upon a heart—just give it time,
and make it a matter of prayer.

Do What You Can

Not everyone can teach a class
or preach to sinful man,
Or visit weak and sickly folk,
or write poems like *I can.*
Not all can travel for the Lord,
to foreign countries go,
Or gently lift the fallen so
the love of Christ they'll know.

But all can hope and all can wait
upon the blessed Lord,
And all can pray that many souls
will search God's holy word.
And all can ask that hindrances
now standing in the way
Will be removed so they can do
more in the coming day.

Gone A-Fishin'

Seven disciples went a-fishin';
Caught no fish throughout the night;
Then a voice from shore called to them
In the glorious morning light.

Seeing Jesus, yet not knowing
Who he was or why he was there,
Seven men listened as he asked them
"Have you any fish to share?"

"No," they answered; "We have nothing."
"Then to the right cast down your net."
Fishes plenty came a swimmin',
More than enough each one would get.

When then for Jesus we go fishin'
Let's listen to Him; let's not fret
If men dismiss our every effort
And leave us weary with empty net.

How Do You Listen?

Jesus loves the ones who hear,
Who quickly listen with the ear
As well as with the soul and heart.
To them rich blessings He'll impart.

Never Alone

If you are in Jesus you're never alone,
No matter how much
or how little you've grown;
For Jesus walks with you
each day and each hour;
He gives what is needed
to live in His pow'r.

If you are in Jesus, then others in Him
Are walking there with you,
whether life's good or grim;
And we should look upwards
and never more fear
For Jesus walks with us,
yes, Jesus is here.

If we are in Jesus we're never alone—
The more we should praise Him,
the less we should groan,
For in Jesus we're circled
with fam'ly and friends
Who know life in Jesus
Brings rich dividends.

Practicing What We Preach

If we who give the message
don't live the message, too,
If we just talk and practice not,
small good those words will do,
For others look not to our speech
nor even to desire,
But good example, godly lives,
which grip souls like a fire.

My Neighbor

I

"So who is my neighbor?" a lawyer one day
Asked Jesus; and He in His usual way
Gave answer in a story, a parable bold,
Of a man who was wounded
and left in the cold.

A priest came that way, but left him lie there,
Then a Levite passed by; neither did he care,
But Providence cared; a Samaritan came
Who stopped when he saw the man
wounded and lame.

With compassion he did what he could;
oil and wine
Were poured in the wounds and
were bound up just fine;
Then onto his strong beast he set the harmed man,
Took him right to an inn, told the keeper his plan.

II

So who is my neighbor? Well,
this story shows
My neighbor is he whose deep

heartache and woes
Are known by me; and to each race or creed
I should do what I can to attend to some need.

So that's what I'll do, because
what's why I'm here—
To help where I'm needed without any fear.
But Jesus, I'm needing Your help ev'ry day
To love all these neighbors
in a most loving way.

The Truth of the Gospel

The truth of the gospel! It has a glad ring,
Obey it and your heart has reason to sing.
Obey it and have all your sins washed away;
Then glory in Jesus, your Savior, today.

Be Tender and Kind

A need there is that we be kind,
To both the seeing and the blind,
To sorrowed hearts and those in sin,
To persons full of guilt within,
To those who on their pillows cry,
To those who on their sick beds lie.

Oh, may we like our Shepherd be,
Speaking with love most tenderly.

Question

It matters not what is your lot
Or how much money you have got;
What is of worth here on this earth,
Is: "Have you experienced the new birth?"

The Little Deed

It's the little deed that people need
To bless their lives each day;
A smile bright, a word just right,
To help along the way.

A helping hand to help them stand
When things get kind of tough;
A word of hope to help them cope
When life seems very rough.

Yes, the little deed is what we need,
It speaks a message true;
For a deed will say in a gracious way,
"I really care for you."

It's Called Worry

With thought and conscience battling
Within, our courage lay
In knowing and believing
That God controls our day.

He knows what we can handle
So He promises to bless
With strength for every battle;
Yet, in our foolishness

And unbelief we'll borrow
More trouble from tomorrow.

Pride is in
Us All

The pride in human beings
is disgusting, I would say,
It seeps into our language
and it creeps into our play;
It boldly guides our thinking
and defies intentions wise,
It wins our motives over
and rewards with sin and lies.

It takes a lot of courage then
to say we <u>really</u> know
We're not even worth a pot of beans—
we've brought our Maker woe;
It takes a hope for better ways,
a hate for actions strange,
A willingness to give up self,
desire to want to change.

But pride which warps our happiness
and leaves us but to grieve
Is nothing new; it came soon after
God made Adam and Eve;
It came when Satan deceived Eve,
which brought about "The Fall."
Yes, pride was there and pride is here,
for pride is in us all.

God is Preparing You

Do you know the special mission
our God has just for _you_?
A very special mission
that only _you_ can do?

Your heartaches, trials—'testings'—
are really for a reason,
They'll make and keep you humble
and last but for a season.

Just seek His leading daily
in big and little things,
Then bless and thank the Father
And praise the King of kings.

Be Content

Thank God for ev'ry morsel, bite,
for ev'ry chair and bed,
For all the clothes you have to wear,
the roof above your head.
Seek not abundance in those things
you handle, touch, and see,
But rather long for spirit'al things
that last eternally.

Vessels in the Making

It is hard to go on with life
and do what needs to be done
when your heart is in pain
or breaking;

However, the Master of the Universe,
continually at work,
has plans for you and I:
vessels in the making;

And you can be sure of this:
He knows what He is about,
having a divine purpose
for each test.

So keep looking up, and trust,
for at the end of each
you shall have victory and joy
and eventually rest.

My New Year's Prayer for You

This coming year I pray that you
Will look to God for what to do,
And give to Him the credit due
For giving life and love to you.

On the

Lighter Side

To every thing there is a season...

A time to weep,

and a time to laugh; a time

to mourn, and a time to dance...

a time to embrace,

and a time to refrain from embracing.

Ecclesiastes 3:1, 4, 5

Dreams

Dreams can be like colored clouds
in the ev'ning sky,
Always changing patterns there,
floating way up high.

Dreams can be like pretty flow'rs
growing for awhile,
Giving beauty to your life,
bringing many a smile.

Dreams can be like stately trees
whose branches bud and swell,
Growing to such lofty heights
you know they're strong and well.

Oh, dreams! How wonderful you are,
your virtues so worthwhile;
Without you life would be humdrum,
lacking verve and style.

Rain

Oh rain, now coming from the sky,
Do tell me please, do tell me why
You're dropping on my bony head
While I am sleeping in my bed.

Doodles

Mind is busy listening,
Phone is to the ear;
Pen is poised within my hand
To write down what I hear.
Then when I least expect it
The pen moves 'round and 'round
And makes the strangest doodles
Without a bit of sound!

The Lazy
Turtle

A turtle too lazy to walk
Was sunning himself on a rock;
When a fly came by
And spit in his eye
He was even too lazy to gawk.

Advice to
My Car

Listen car, and listen well
To this advice I have to tell:
If you keep smoking as you do,
You'll never live to twenty-two.

Hug a Tree

Do hug a tree,
because you see,
They're quite like you
and quite like me;
They need our love and affection, too.

They will better grow
with much less woe,
For loving hugs,
now you must know,
Make all the "huggees" feel like new.

I Marvel at
Man

I marvel at man, what he can do
with cars that 'die', to make them 'new'.
Just give him some tools and time and space
and he, with grease all over his face
And hands and clothes—in no time at all
will proudly say, with stature tall,
"I have it running like a clock.
You want a ride around the block?"
And in he hops, you at his side.
What wonderment! What glorious pride!
I marvel, yes, I surely do
how man can make a wreck like new.

Poor Writer's Mate

Papers! Papers! Everywhere!
Under the bed and on the chair;
In every room and cupboard, too,
Oh, what's a writer's mate to do?

Poor writer's mate who thinks it's right
To have all papers out of sight;
Well, what's a writer's mate to do?
Of course, become a writer, too!

Through the Seasons

Through the seasons, God, my might,
Has helped me see and helped me fight
The many foes within, without
And kept my soul in ev'ry bout.

Through the seasons, Christ my hope,
Has given strength to help me cope;
He's blessed my life and made me whole
And provided needs for body and soul.

Through the seasons, the Spirit true
Has lived within and helped me do

The many things I should and would,
Like, be to others kind and good.

Yes, through the seasons, from the hand
Of our Heav'nly Father ever so grand,
Come blessings rich; I plan to praise
His holy name throughout my days.

Advice to Myself

Open your eyes and see what you see:
Rocks on the road and sap on the tree,
Beautiful vines twining this way and that,
Flowers in bloom,
the log where you sat.

Open your ears and hear what you hear:
Birds singing sweetly without any fear,
Cars on the highway, a plane in the sky,
The gentle wind blowing,
a train passing by.

Open your senses and feel what you feel:
Open your nostrils and smell what is real;
Look all around and thank God for His love,
For He's given these blessings
from heaven above.

My World

My world is full of beautiful trees;
Of animals, mountains, and seas;
It's full of treasures in the sand,
Of thrilling sights on every hand.

It's filled with power, praise, and prayer,
Of happy folk who love and care;
It's full of noble thoughts and song
That help me stay where I belong!

Praise God my world (not silver lined)
Is many things all intertwined,
To help prepare the likes of me
To live with Him eternally.

When I see Old Glory Fly

My eyes are fastened to it
as it flutters in the breeze;
My heart pounds sometimes wildly
and weak become my knees.

Then comes to mind the flag salute,
the happy memory
When I was younger and well taught—
to honor it, you see.

And so I thrill to see it there,
on a flag-pole way up high,
And oft I end up praying when
I see Old Glory fly.

Words

Words, words
stabbing words
pounding, hounding
wounding me, and more
piercing to the core;
Taking my breath
bringing death
to happy dreams
through ugly schemes!
Forgive their words, O Lord.

Words, words
wondrous words
sifting, lifting
giving hope and wings
to noble dreams and things;
Delighting the inner soul
shaping plan and goal,
and at length
giving needed strength.
Thank you, Lord, for words.

"A" is for Apple

Munchy, crunchy, sweet and good,
Apples are a wondrous food;
Good for teeth and good for gums,
Help for lingering doldrums.

When to eat the apple sweet?
Eat it in the place of meat;
Eat it when from sleep you rise;
Before bedtime is also wise.

Scorn ye not the apple fine,
But on it daily sup or dine;
Juice or solid—relish it—
For apples make one fine and fit.

My Secret

I went to my room one fine morning
To study about a few things,
But birds chirping songs at my window
And moths with brown fuzz on their wings
Kept me looking out and day dreaming
About everything under the sun,
Except what I planned there to study—
So nothing, but nothing, got done!

The time! How it sped by and traveled
While doing thing I liked to do;
Then a thought got me really excited,
For a "secret" I suddenly knew!
I'd make things, like work and like study,
And things I did not think were fun,
Exciting, and yes, interesting,
And then I would get those things done!

So a chart I made up for my study;
A good one, just suited for me;
I smiled as I now comprehended
My very own teacher I'd be.
I chose my most favorite subjects,
Then studied for a half, then an hour,
And was pleased, very pleased to discover
Self-discipline does give one power.

Silly Questions

Have you ever felt a fuzzy flute
sharp squash or corky corn?
Have you ever heard a squeaky snake
bubbly bangs or a hummer horn?
Have you every seen a haggard ham
a doggie drum or a stripped sty?
You haven't? Oh, what a shame!
But then, neither have I!

CPSIA information can be obtained at www.ICGtesting.com
Printed in the USA
LVOW10s0520040614

388541LV00002B/3/P